Solana Back Online: The Rise of Solana and the Decentralized Future

Louis E. Trottier

TABLE OF CONTENTS

CHAPTER 1

INTRODUCTION

Solana (SOL): What Is It?

A blockchain platform called Solana is intended to provide scalable, decentralized apps. Established in 2017, the project is being managed as an open-source endeavor by the Geneva-based Solana Foundation, with Solana Labs in San Francisco responsible for building the blockchain.

Compared to competing blockchains like Ethereum, Solana processes transactions more quickly and charges much lower fees for each transaction. The cryptocurrency known as Solana (SOL), which is based on the Solana blockchain, surged by about 12,000% in 2021 and, at one point, had a market valuation of over $75 billion, making it one of the biggest at the time.

Notwithstanding its widespread use, SOL was not spared from the 2022 cryptocurrency apocalypse. SOL's market value has decreased to almost $3.63 billion on December 29, 2022. It had regained over half of its lost market capitalization after a year.

ESSENTIAL NOTES

- A blockchain platform called Solana is intended to provide scalable, decentralized apps.
- Compared to competing blockchains like Ethereum, Solana has a far higher transaction processing rate and reduced transaction costs.
- A proof-of-history (PoH) method, which uses hashed timestamps to confirm when transactions occur, enhances the proof-of-stake (PoS) blockchain found in Solana.

SOLANA'S HISTORY

Co-founder of Solana Anatoly Yakovenko has worked with industry leaders in technology, including Qualcomm Incorporated (QCOM), in the area of distributed systems architecture. Through this experience, he realized that a dependable clock makes network synchronization easier. Once that happens, the network's speed will increase dramatically, with bandwidth serving as the sole limit.

According to Yakovenko's theory, using proof-of-history will significantly accelerate blockchain systems like Bitcoin and Ethereum in comparison to blockchain systems without clocks. These systems found it difficult to grow over 15 transactions per second (TPS) globally, which is a small amount of the throughput managed by centralized payment systems like Visa (V), which may reach up to 65,000 TPS at peak times.

This obstacle is overcome by Yakavenko's proof-of-history, which enables each node in the network to depend on the time that has been recorded.

CONCEPT OF PROOF-OF-HISTORY

In November 2017, Yakovenko released a white paper outlining the proof-of-history (PoH) idea. PoH is used to encode the passage of time into a ledger and enables the blockchain to attain consensus by confirming the interval between occurrences.

Yakovenko writes in the white paper that blockchains that were accessible to the general public at the time did not depend on time, as each node in the network used its local clock and was unaware of the clocks of any other nodes in the network. Because there was no reliable source of time (a defined clock), there was no assurance that other network participants would use a message timestamp to accept or reject messages in the same way.

Yakovenko enlisted five more people in 2018 to help co-found the Loom project. They renamed the project "Solana," after the co-founders' former home, a tiny beach town outside San Diego, to avoid confusion with another Ethereum-based project of the same name.

The project was scaled up to operate on cloud-based networks in June 2018, and a month later, the business released a public test net that could accommodate 250,000 TPS bursts.

At an average cost of $0.00025 for each transaction, Solana has completed over 253 billion transactions by December 12, 2023.

Like Ethereum's ERC-20, Solana has its tokenization standard called SPL Token.

The Technology of Solana

Blockchain software-induced speed constraints are eliminated by Solana's architecture via the usage of algorithms. It is decentralized, safe, and scalable as a result. Theoretically, its design can support up to 28.4 million TPS on a 40-gigabit network and a maximum of 710,000 TPS on a normal gigabit network.

The consensus models used by Solana's blockchain are proof-of-stake (PoS) and proof-of-history (PoH). Timestamped and swiftly validated transactions are made possible via PoS, which enables validators—those who check transactions recorded to the blockchain ledger—to verify transactions depending on the number of coins or tokens they own.

Solana employs validator clusters—groups of validators that collaborate to process transactions—instead of validator nodes.
Ethereum vs. Solana

Solana has inevitably been compared to Ethereum, the top blockchain for decentralized apps (dApps), given its quickly growing ecosystem and adaptability:
Ethereum and Solana both support smart contracts, which are essential for the operation of cutting-edge applications like non-fungible tokens (NFTs) and decentralized finance (DeFi).

Consensus: Solana and Ethereum both use proof-of-stake (PoS) consensus, in which participants may earn incentives for supporting the blockchain by staking their cryptocurrency as collateral. By including PoH as well, Solana enhances PoS.

Speed: In 2021, Solana generated a lot of excitement because of its clear advantages over Ethereum in terms of transaction fees and processing speed. As of December 12, 2023, Solana was processing over 2,700 transactions per second, with an average transaction cost of $0.00025. Ethereum, on the other hand, has a throughput of less than 15 TPS and charges an average of $2.62 for transactions.

Ethereum Updates

With its extensive ecosystem and first-mover advantage, Ethereum is the second most valuable cryptocurrency behind Bitcoin. Ethereum's blockchain is now more scalable, secure, and sustainable thanks to its 2022 update, which combined its Beacon Chain and Mainnet Chain. Sharding will be included in a later version, which will drastically cut down on transaction times and network congestion. We're not sure how Solana will respond to these advancements yet.

KEY QUESTIONS

Is Fractional Amounts Available for Solana's SOL Token?

Imports, which are fractional quantities of SOLs, have a value of 0.000000001 SOL. The Lamports have the name of Leslie Lamport, a computer scientist well recognized for his contributions to distributed systems, who was Solana's greatest technological influence.

How Many SOL Tokens Are in Use Right Now?

SOL tokens are abundant in Solana's possession. On December 12, 2023, there were 426 million SOL in circulation.

Where Does Solana Stand in the Crypto Industry?

On December 12, 2023, Solana ranked sixth among cryptocurrencies according to market capitalization. Among its most formidable competitors were XRP, Tether, BNB, Ethereum, and Bitcoin.

CHAPTER 2

WHAT MAKES SOLANA THE FIRST WEB-SCALE BLOCKCHAIN: 8 INNOVATIONS

Anatoly Yakovenko, the company's creator, came up with the idea for Solana in 2017 while looking for a method to make a decentralized network of nodes function on par with a single node. This is a feature that none of the main blockchains have even approached. Solana's goal is to do this.

About ten transactions per second (TPS) are supported by proof-of-work systems like Ethereum and Bitcoin. Systems that handle 1,000 TPS or more with 100–200 nodes are practical Byzantine Fault Tolerance-based (PBFT) Proof of Stake (PoS) systems, such as Tendermint. As of the current testnet iterations, Solana, a PoS blockchain analogous to PBFT, supports up to 50,000 TPS with more than 200 nodes, making it the most performant blockchain and the first web-scale decentralized network in history.

The Solana team, which is made up of tech pioneers from Qualcomm, Intel, Netscape, and Google, has been working nonstop to develop the technology needed to make Solana work with these ground-breaking performance criteria ever since it was founded.

The Solana team created eight essential technologies to build a permissionless, decentralized network with performance comparable to a single node:

1. The Proof of History (POH) clock is a precursor to consensus.
2. Tower BFT is PBFT with PoH optimization;
3. Turbine: a protocol for block propagation;

4. Gulf Stream: a transaction forwarding protocol without a mempool;
5. Sealevel: Run-time of parallel smart contracts;
6. Pipelining: A Transaction Processing Unit for validation optimization
7. Cloudbreak: Horizontally-Scaled Accounts Database and
8. Archivers: Distributed ledger storage

Each of the aforementioned will be briefly explained in this article. We've also prepared thorough explainers for each, which you can see by clicking the links above if you want to know more.

Proof of History

If the overall performance of a blockchain network is to equal that of a single node, then computing rather than bandwidth must be the barrier. We must first optimize network node communication to do this.

Blockchain-based networks and wireless cellular networks are quite similar in that they have historically prioritized network communication optimization. Telecom corporations required "multiple access technologies" to jam as many phone calls as possible into a single radio frequency since, at scale, no single radio tower has the bandwidth to provide every cell phone its radio frequency to broadcast on.

One of the key technologies that allowed for tremendous scalability in cellular networks is Time Division Multiple Access (TDMA). According to TDMA specifications, towers must provide a time slot for each radio frequency and split them up. The cell tower gives the network a globally accessible clock in this way. Allowing each frequency to handle several simultaneous data channels and reducing interference from numerous phones broadcasting on the same frequency at the same time, greatly enhances the scalability of limited bandwidth.

Blockchain-based networks of today suffer from a clock issue. Every time they manufacture a new brick, their clocks "tick." Since a single block of Ethereum may only contain so much data, that occurs once every fifteen seconds. A clock with sub-second granularity that all validating nodes agree upon would be the TDMA counterpart for blockchain-based networks, enabling them to process transactions more quickly.

Proof of History (POH), a globally accessible, permissionless source of time on the network that operates before consensus, is the fundamental innovation of Solana. POH is not an anti-Sybil mechanism or consensus procedure. Instead, POH addresses the clock issue.

Because each Solana validator encodes the passage of time in a straightforward SHA-256, sequential-hashing verifiable delay function (VDF), each validator maintains its clock independently of other blockchains, which need validators to communicate with one another to agree that time has passed. For unpredictability, Solana does not use a VDF. Rather, every validator keeps track of time using the VDF. Leader selection is done in advance for a whole epoch as every validator keeps track of time on its clock.

The timetable for an epoch spans thousands of blocks, much as that of tendermint. The network, in contrast to Tendermint, never waits for a failing node. To demonstrate that it has obtained its slot for transmitting a block and validators, each validator executes the VDF. Because the block producer is paid for creating a block, each validator is rewarded for their efforts.

No matter the state of the network, leaders keep rotating, and the network as a whole advances thanks to Proof of History. In other words, the network never shuts down. Without any of the validators communicating with one another, the network might decide to rotate the validators. This change is little yet significant. There isn't a similar mechanism on any other blockchain. In all other chains, decision-making by validators requires communication. Decisions on leader rotation are made asynchronously in Solana.

This fundamental breakthrough expanded the design area upward in the stack. POH gives Solana the ability to optimize for block time (800 ms), block propagation (log 200 n), throughput (50 − 80 = K TPS), and ledger storage (petabytes) accessible on the network, in addition to giving a clock that may be used for timestamping.

Tower BFT

Solana utilizes Tower Consensus, a consensus method akin to PBFT and created especially to benefit from the synchronized clock, atop Proof of History. Tower Consensus values liveliness above consistency, in contrast to PBFT. Similar to PBFT, nodes raise their timeouts exponentially to reach a consensus; however, because the ledger is a trustless source of time, nodes can watch and analyze the timeouts of every other validator in the network. To comprehend better, let's look at an example:

Envision yourself on an island where a thumb drive-containing bottle drifts past. There is a Solana ledger inside the disk. Simply examining the ledger reveals that every node can determine the number of validators in use, their current status, and, most importantly, the timeouts they have committed to each block inside the network. Without any peer-to-peer communications, a validator may decide whether to cast a vote based only on the data structure, and the network can reach a consensus.

Turbine

Irrespective of agreement, Solana can optimize block transmission via the network since its consensus layer does not rely on peer-to-peer messaging. BitTorrent is a major source of inspiration for Solana's block-propagation method, Turbine. A block is divided into smaller packets and spread out over a wide range of randomly selected peers as it is broadcast, accompanied byby erasure codes. The network's second layer can span 40,000 validators with a fan-out of 200. This means that blocks with a $\log 200(n)$ effect to finality may be propagated by validators. Replication can be completed in 400 ms and finality in 500 ms for a 40,000-node40,000-node network, assuming that each connection takes 100 ms.

The fanout system has to be error-proof. Therefore, validators provide a certain level of fault tolerance by encrypting data using Reed-Solomon erasure codes.

Gulf Stream

Mempool management is a new class of problems in high-speed networks that other chains don't need to deal with. Pushing transaction caching and forwarding to the network's edge is how Gulf Stream operates. Clients and validators transmit transactions to the anticipated leader ahead of time since every validator is aware of the order of the incoming leaders in the Solana architecture.

As a result, validators may process transactions ahead of schedule, cut down on confirmation delays, swap leaders more quickly, and ease the load on their memory caused by the unconfirmed transaction pool.

Wallets and other clients sign transactions that make use of a certain block-hash. Clients choose a recently generated block-hash that has been verified in full by the network. About every 800 ms, a new block is offered, and each new block needs a progressively longer wait to unroll. In the worst scenario, a completely verified block-hash is 32 blocks old based on our default timeout curve. With 800 ms block times, it works out to 25.6 seconds.

A transaction is sent to one of the future leaders by the validator once it has been sent to any validator. Subscribers to transaction confirmations from validators are available. Clients are aware that a block-hash has a fixed expiration date or that the network has validated the transaction. Clients may now sign transactions that are certain to succeed or fail. Clients are guaranteed that a transaction is invalid and won't be processed on the chain once the network reaches a point when the blockhash to which it relates has expired.

Sealevel

We developed Sealevel, a hyper-parallelized transaction processing engine that can expand horizontally across GPUs and SSDs, to benefit from Solana's high-performance network. Be aware that single-threaded processors power every other blockchain. The only chain that allows for simultaneous transaction execution on a single shard rather than merely signature verification is Solana.

This problem's solution depends extensively on the scatter-gather operating system driver approach. Transactions declare in advance the states they will read and write while they are in operation. The runtime may optimize the scheduling of reads and writes to the state over a range of RAID 0 SSDs by identifying all non-overlapping state transition functions that occur in a block and executing them in parallel. This process is known as parallel execution.

Sealevel is a virtual machine (VM) that arranges transactions; however, it does not perform transaction execution inside the VM. Rather, Berkeley Packet Filter (BPF), an industry-proven bytecode intended for high-performance packet filters, is used by Sealevel to forward transactions to native hardware execution. Since the early 1990s, this bytecode has been refined and implemented in millions of switches throughout the globe, enabling them to manage 60 million packets per second on a 40-gigabit network inside a single switch.

Our network will quadruple in processing capability each time Nvidia doubles the number of accessible SIMD lanes. Because they are by nature single-threaded machines, almost all other blockchains are never able to scale in this manner.

We provide developers with an excellent set of tools to construct high-performance

C/C++ and Rust smart contracts that run on GPUs using LLVM, the same compiler that targets WASM. Even though Solana doesn't use WASM, programmers may easily recompile C and Rust code meant for WASM compilers using the Solana compiler.

As a result, programmers may quickly move their apps from other significant WASM chains, such as Ethereum 2.0, Dfinity, EOS, and Polkadot.

The software design of Ethereum has a history of including problems. Two pertinent instances:

- Multiple Delegate Call parity hacks
- The "call" method of the DAO reentrancy problem

Just as it is feasible to develop complicated software in C without memory protection, it is also possible to build secure Solidity code. However, the verification of complicated software's behavior grows geometrically harder the longer risky behavior is simple to create and difficult to detect. This issue was identified early on by both the Libra team and Solana, who created designs that maintain a rigid division of state across various modules.

Scripts and Resources were first presented as high-level ideas by the Move language. Both mesh well with the Solana Sealevel Runtime and our current native application architecture. Our objective is to enable Move as a first-level language such that Resources may be produced and built using Move or our own native Rust ABI without sacrificing security or performance. Resources will then act like native Solana applications.

Pipelining

is used as a Transaction Processing Unit to optimize validation

The Solana network's transaction validation procedure heavily utilizes pipelining, an efficiency often seen in CPU architecture.

When a stream of input data has to be processed via a series of stages and separate hardware is in charge of each step, pipelining is an acceptable approach.

Transaction Processing Units, or pipeline mechanisms, advance via Data Fetching at the kernel level, Signature Verification at the GPU level, Banking at the CPU level, and Writing at the kernel space on the Solana network. The TPU has already fetched the subsequent batch of packets, confirmed the signers' identities, and started awarding tokens by the time it begins sending blocks to the validators.

The Solana TPU can work on 50,000 transactions at once at any one time because of the GPU parallelization in this four-stage pipeline. All of this is possible with a computer that costs less than $5,000 off the shelf. This GPU offloading into Solana's TPU may impact the single-node efficiency of the network.

Cloudbreak

Scaling computing just isn't enough. Account tracking memory rapidly becomes a barrier in terms of size and access performance. For instance, it's well known that LevelDB, the local database engine used by many contemporary chains, has a maximum throughput of 5,000 TPS.

Keeping the global state in RAM is an amateurish fix. It is unreasonable to anticipate that consumer-grade computers would have enough RAM to store the whole world's state, however. We created Cloudbreak, a state architecture optimized for simultaneous reads and writes dispersed across a RAID 0 configuration of SSDs, specifically for Solana. Every extra disk increases the amount of storage that on-chain applications can access and the number of concurrent reads and writes that programs can carry out at the same time.

This architecture facilitates AOT (Ahead Of Time) transaction execution when combined with our transaction design. When a validator notices a transaction, Sealevel may begin pre-fetching all of the accounts from disk and getting the runtime ready for use. Block producers and validators may even begin processing transactions before the transactions are encoded into a block, enabling us to further reduce confirmation latencies and block times.

Archivers

A blockchain network will produce 4 petabytes of data annually for the ledger at 1GBPS. Data storage would swiftly take the lead in centralization, negating the whole point of using blockchain technology.

On Solana, a network of nodes known as Archivers handles data storage instead of validators. Archivists don't take part in group discussions. The state's past is erased and divided into several fragments. Parts of the state are preserved by archivists. The network will periodically request proof from the Archivers that they are saving the data that they are meant to. Proofs of Replication (PoRep), which are mostly derived from Filecoin, are used by Solana.

Proof of History, our clock before consensus, allows us to optimize the creation of PoReps. To provide lightweight proof that portions of the ledger have been copied, archiver nodes which do not engage in consensus use PoH. Validators may then check these proofs in extremely large batches over several GPUs.

Laptops and other lightweight nodes may serve as archivers. A network of archivers equipped with redundancy and erasure codes can ensure data availability better than anything AWS or GCE could ever hope to deliver.

CHAPTER 3

SHUT DOWN SOLANA IS BACK UP, WHAT BROUGHT IT DOWN

Tuesday saw another interruption on the Solana network, bringing its first outage-free anniversary dangerously close.
After five hours of outage, developers released a fix and brought the network back up.

Network activity is increasing even though there have been previous interruptions.
According to a network status report, Solana's blockchain is now executing transactions again after a "major outage" that stopped it for around five hours on Tuesday.

The network ceased generating transaction blocks at about 9:52 AM GMT, which marked the start of today's (6 February 2024) outage.

The Solana team quickly recognized the problem and said that engineers were trying to get the service back up and running.

The network was restarted at about 2:47 PM GMT after engineers published a new software patch for the blockchain that addressed the issue.

Solana validator Stakewiz designed a dashboard that lets users keep an eye on the process.

When the progress indicator on the dashboard reached 80%, which is the cutoff point for the network to resume in terms of chatter between active validators, the network restarted.

In Solana, network users employ gossip as a communication technique. When Solana's blockchain is operating correctly, gossip is how data is exchanged between network nodes.

The network is operational once again, according to the Solana Beach dashboard, which serves as a gateway for Solana measurements.

This time, what brought Solana down?

Although the chain is back up, the reason for today's failure is yet unknown to the general public.

The Solana team said via its X account that "core contributors are working on a root cause report, which will be made available once complete." DL News reached out to Solana's core team members for comment, but they did not immediately answer.

Even while Solana has seen several network issues of differing magnitude over the last three years, the disruption that occurred today ended the blockchain's almost one-year-long streak of 0% downtime.

The most recent network outage, which lasted over two days, occurred on February 25, 2023. The network was overloaded with transactions as a result of a viral NFT mint, which was the source of that problem.

The blockchain is seeing a strong comeback; since October of last year, the value of the DeFi market has quadrupled to $1.7 billion. This coincides with Tuesday's outage.

Airdrop and meme currency speculation have been the main drivers of this expansion, which has led to a wave of liquidity migration from other blockchains, notably Ethereum.

www.ingramcontent.com/pod-product-compliance
Lightning Source LLC
LaVergne TN
LVHW051649050326
832903LV00034B/4772